Unbelievable Pictures and Facts About German Shepherds

By: Olivia Greenwood

Introduction

German shepherds are wonderful dogs to have as pets. They make a fantastic addition to the family, plus they are super smart. They are also very useful as working dogs and they can fulfill many different roles. Today you will have the opportunity to learn all about these truly amazing dogs.

How popular are German shepherds in America?

It may not come as a surprise to you but German shepherd dogs are very popular in America. They are one of the most popular dog breeds of all time.

Are any sports unique to the German shepherd?

Back in the days, there was one sport which was created specifically for German shepherds. The name of this sport was Schutzhund.

Exactly how do people describe the German shepherd?

These dogs are known for many things. They are described by people as "highly intelligent", "very loyal" and "brave".

Are German shepherds more at risk for anything?

Unfortunately, German shepherds are at high risk for pituitary dwarfism. This is a problem which is very common to the German shepherd breed. This condition involves a growth hormone deficiency and can result in a wide variety of problems.

What type of noses do German shepherds have?

German shepherds have very powerful noses. Their sense of smell and abilities because of this is very impressive. They are known as being one of the dogs with the best sense of smell.

Is the German shepherd breed an intelligent breed?

There is absolutely no doubt about it. German Shepherds are highly intelligent. In fact, they are said to be the third smartest dog breed in the world.

Do these dogs need to be washed frequently?

Fortunately for German shepherd owners, it is not necessary to wash these dogs very often. Although they do need to be groomed every single day because of their coat which sheds hair on a very regular basis.

What kind of coats do German shepherd dogs have?

The coat of a German shepherd dog has the tendency to shed for the entire year. There is no time of the year when their coat is not shedding. They have a thick double layer type of coat.

Which specific traits do people recognize in the German shepherd?

These dogs have been known to perform all sorts of heroic acts over the years. They have defended their owners, saved their owners and even taken bullets for them. They constantly throughout the years have performed remarkable acts of kindness and bravery.

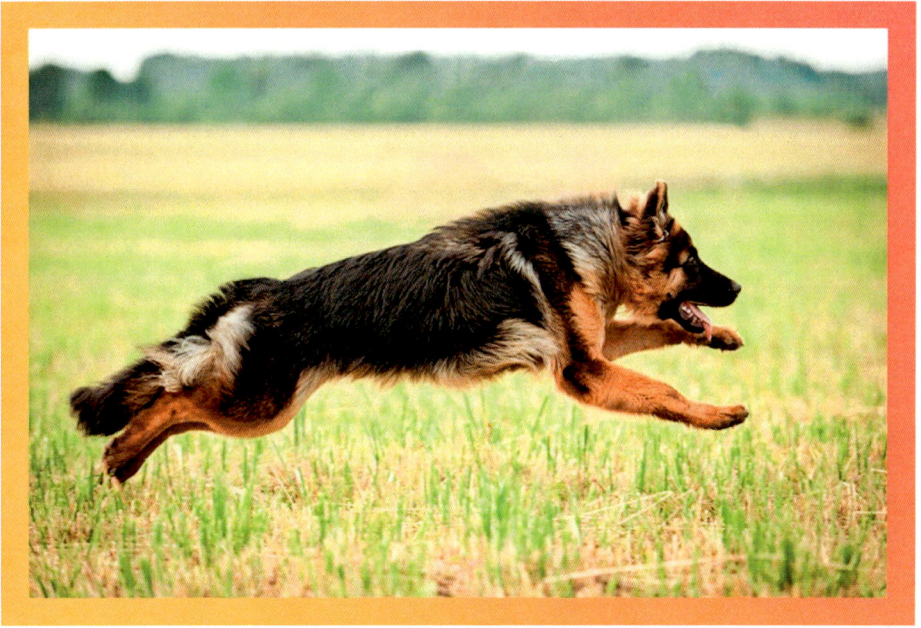

Are German shepherds compliant dogs?

The answer is yes. German shepherds are extremely compliant dogs. For the majority of the time, they pick up and learn commands extremely easily and quickly.

Do German shepherds learn quickly?

German shepherds are remarkable dogs. They have the ability to learn things really quickly. After only 5 repetitions they are able to learn a command. There have been cases of German shepherds who learn more than 100 commands in the first year of life.

Does the German shepherd dog have a powerful bite?

German shepherds have a tendency to have a very strong bite. They can really bite with huge amounts of force. Their bite is much more powerful and forceful than that of human beings.

Have there been any German shepherds in Hollywood?

Have you ever heard of Rin Tin Tin? He was a very famous German shepherd dog. He was famous in Hollywood and he has been in over 26 movies.

Do police officers make use of German shepherds?

The answer is a big yes. German Shepherds are extremely intelligent dogs who are also very agile. For these reasons, they make excellent police dogs. They have been assisting police forces from around the world for many years.

Have any trends begun from the German shepherd?

You may be totally amazed to discover that the very first seeing eye dog in the entire world was a beautiful German shepherd. His name was Buddy and this was back in the 1920s. This started the seeing eye dog movement that we know today.

How many years do German shepherds live up until?

The average lifespan of a German shepherd is anything from 9 to 13 years of age. They have a moderately long lifespan in comparison to other dogs.

Which colors do German shepherds come in?

These beautiful dogs come in a variety of colors. The colors range from black to tan. You get all sorts of colors and color combinations.

Which physical features are these dogs known for?

The one physical feature that all German shepherds are known for, is their ears. When they are puppies their ears have a strong tendency to flop down. However, when they get older their ears have a tendency to stick up.

What is the proper name given to this breed of dog?

There is actually an official name for the German shepherd breed. The official name is the German shepherd dog. It is important to understand that the word dog is used at the end of this name.

Who was the first person to create the German shepherd breed?

Back in the history books, way back in 1889, there was a man named How Max Von Stephanitz. Max was the first person to discover the German shepherd and he started to breed more of them. He is known throughout the world as the father of this amazing dog breed.

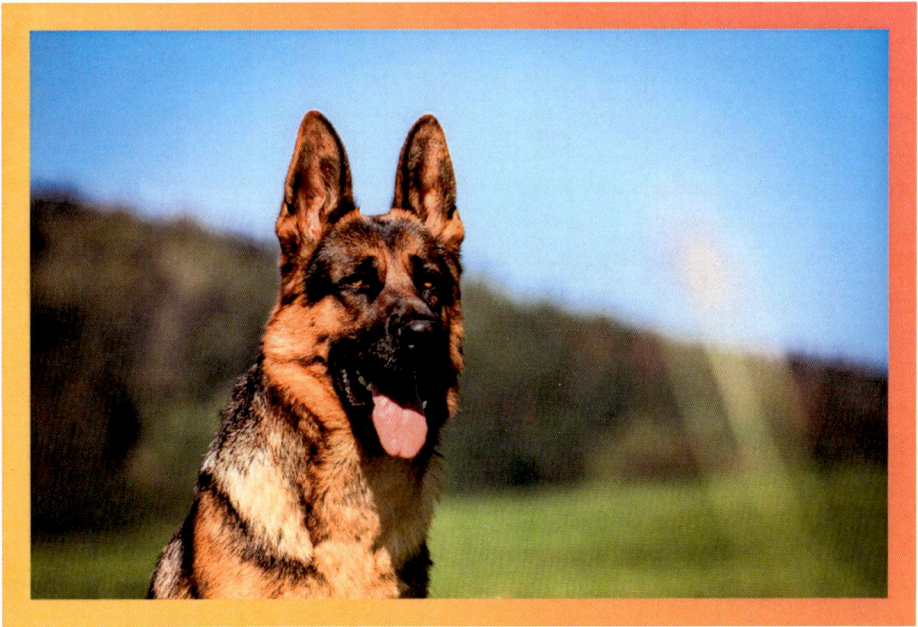

Made in United States
North Haven, CT
20 November 2021